TITANIC
Lost and saved

WHITE STAR LINE

TITANIC

19   12

Brian Moses

First published in 2011 by Wayland
Copyright © Wayland 2011

Wayland
338 Euston Road
London NW1 3BH

Wayland Australia
Level 17/207 Kent Street
Sydney, NSW 2000

Design: Elaine Wilkinson
Editor: Victoria Brooker

Picture Acknowledgments: Main cover, title page and page 16
(bottom) Mary Evans Picture Library; menu ©2002 Topham/PA
TopFoto.co.uk; coins Brendan Howard/Shutterstock; key and
trinket box: Shutterstock;1(left), 5 Mary Evans Picture Library (right)
© Ocean/Corbis; 3 (left) Shutterstock, (right) Rob Kemp/Shutterstock;
(bottom) Plechi/Shutterstock; 8 (top)Mary Evans/Onslow Auctions
Limited; 9 (top) ©Roger-Viollet/TopFoto.co.uk; 10 (top) TopFoto.co.uk;
11 (top) ©2003 Topham Picturepoint /TopFoto.co.uk; 12 (top) ©2002
Topham/PA TopFoto.co.uk, (bottom) Mary Evans/Onslow Auctions
Limited; 13 (top) Mary Evans/Onslow Auctions Limited; 13 (top) Mary Evans/Onslow Auctions Limited (bottom) TopFoto.
co.uk; 14 (top) ©2003 Topham Picturepoint/TopFoto.co.uk; 15 (bottom) © The Mariners' Museum/CORBIS; 16 (top)
Topfoto.co.uk (bottom) Mary Evans; 17 (top) ©2004 Topham Picturepoint/TopFoto.co.uk; (middle) Adrian Stuart; 23 (top)
fsquared limited /shutterstock, (bottom) Rob Stark/Shutterstock; 25 (top) ©2003 Topham Picturepoint/TopFoto.co.uk; 28
(top) ©ullsteinbild/TopFoto co.uk (bottom) ARPL/HIP/TopFoto.co.uk ; 30 (top) Willy Stower, (bottom) Valeriy Lebedev
/Shutterstock; 31 (middle): ©ullsteinbild/TopFoto.co.uk, (bottom) Rob Kemp/Shutterstock; 32 ©TopFoto.co.uk; 34 ©
Bettmann/CORBIS; 36 (bottom) TopFoto.co.uk; 38 © Bettmann/CORBIS; 39 (top) Roger-Viollet/Topfoto.co.uk, (middle)
TopFoto.co.uk, (bottom right) Jill Battaglia/shutterstock; 41 ©1999 Topham Picturepoint/TopFoto.co.uk; 42 TopFoto.co.uk;
43 (top) ©2002 Topham Picturepoint/TopFoto.co.uk; 44 (bottom) ©2004 TopFoto/UPP; 45 ©2003 Topham Picturepoint/
TopFoto.co.uk

Every attempt has been made to clear copyright for this edition. Should there be any inadvertent omission
please apply to the publisher for rectification.

British Library Cataloguing in Publication Data
  Moses, Brian, 1950-
  Titanic lost and saved.
  1. Titanic (Steamship)--Juvenile literature.
  2. Shipwrecks--North Atlantic Ocean--History--
  20th century--Juvenile literature.
  I. Title
  910.9'1634-dc22
  ISBN: 978 0 7502 6666 6

Printed in China

Wayland is a division of Hachette Children's Books, an Hachette UK company.
www.hachette.co.uk

Note: There are some discrepancies in passenger records due to cancelled trips, transfers
to other ships and some passengers and crew simply being left behind. Some passengers
traded or sold their boarding passes, and names of alternate passengers were never recorded.

Contents

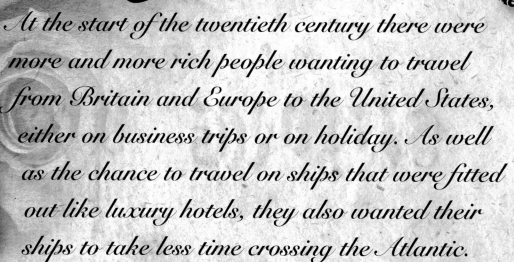

Ship of Dreams

At the start of the twentieth century there were more and more rich people wanting to travel from Britain and Europe to the United States, either on business trips or on holiday. As well as the chance to travel on ships that were fitted out like luxury hotels, they also wanted their ships to take less time crossing the Atlantic.

Shipping companies such as Cunard started building larger and faster ships, and in September 1907 they launched the *Mauretania* and the *Lusitania*. These could cross the Atlantic in less than six days.

J. Bruce Ismay was the owner of the shipping company, the White Star Line. He was upset about all the publicity Cunard were getting with their latest ships and he asked naval architect Thomas Andrews to design three new ships, bigger and better than anything that had been built before. They were to be called *Olympic, Titanic* and *Gigantic* (later to be renamed *Britannic*).

J. Bruce Ismay had a central role in the Titanic's story.

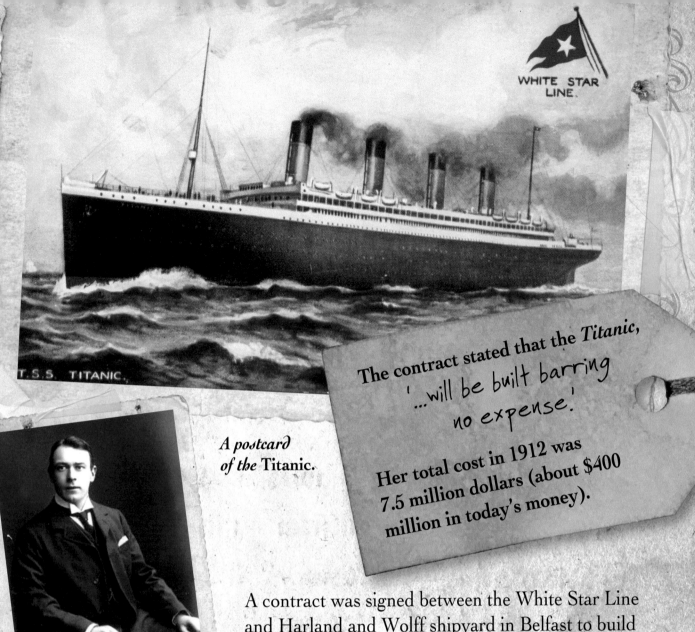

T.S.S. TITANIC.

*A postcard
of the* Titanic.

*Thomas Andrews believed
his ship to be unsinkable.*

The contract stated that the *Titanic,*
'...will be built barring
no expense.'

Her total cost in 1912 was
7.5 million dollars (about $400
million in today's money).

A contract was signed between the White Star Line
and Harland and Wolff shipyard in Belfast to build
all three ships, and work started first on the *Olympic.*
It was thought that any lessons learnt from the
building of the first ship could be useful in the
construction of the *Titanic,* with the aim of making her
the biggest, fastest and most luxurious ship of her day.

Titanic's Dimensions

Length: 269 metres
Width: 27.8 metres
Height from keel to navigating bridge: 31.5 metres
Gross tonnage: 45,000 tonnes
Speed: 21 knots
Total capacity: 3547 passengers

Building the Titanic

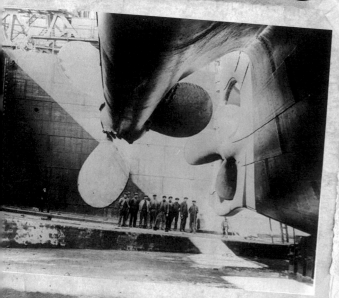

These men standing close to the Titanic's propeller give some idea as to how huge she was.

The Titanic was constructed under the world's largest gantry at Harland and Wolff's Queen's Island. Building started in the spring of 1909 and more than 10,000 men worked for three years on the ship's hull and interiors.

The *Titanic* was built alongside the *Olympic*. Both ships were so huge that each took up the space of two ordinary ships. The keel of the ship was built first. This runs the length of the ship along the bottom in its very centre. The *Titanic* had a double-plated bottom, about 1.65m thick along her length, and 30cm thicker for the engine room. About 500,000 rivets were needed for the ship's double bottom.

The Titanic and Olympic were built side by side at Queen's Island shipyard in Belfast.

Bulkheads divided the *Titanic* into 16 watertight compartments with electrically-controlled doors that would close automatically when the water level reached a certain height. The *Titanic* was, in the words of J. Bruce Ismay, '...especially constructed to float with her two largest watertight compartments full of water.'

The **Titanic** *in Belfast just prior to her launch.*

Next the hull framework was attached followed by the hull plates. The *Titanic* needed 1,200 tons of rivets for its hull and at last the ship was starting to look like a ship.

Twenty horses were needed to pull each one of the Titanic's 15-ton anchors on a wagon through Belfast to the shipyard.

A view of the unpainted **Titanic**.

Belfast Launch Day:
31 May 1911

It took just 62 seconds for the Titanic to be launched as she slid into the water along greased runners. A crowd of 10,000 gathered to watch including J. Bruce Ismay and his family and the Titanic's architect Thomas Andrews. Once the ship reached the water her progress was halted by huge chains.

Poster advertising the Titanic's homeward trip.

Finishing the *Titanic* would take another 10 months. Machinery such as engines, funnels and boilers were winched onto the ship once she was at sea using floating cranes. The ship's 10 decks were also completed. Passenger accommodation would be on the upper seven decks - the Promenade, Bridge, Shelter, Saloon, Upper, Middle and Lower. The three remaining decks were for cargo and machinery.

White Star Line poster for the world's largest liner.

The *Titanic* was fitted out with staircases, including the magnificent Grand Staircase, electric lifts and refrigeration units. It also had wood panelling and carpeting in the first-class areas.

Titanic's *first-class lounge*.

'Fog signals were exploded, the sirens in the Lough shrieked and a great cheer went up as the leviathan glided gracefully into the waters of the Lagan.'
Sunday Independent, 1911

'There had been economy only in one thing by those who built the ship and furnished her. They had economised in boats and rafts. It seemed so foolish to carry boats when the 'Titanic' was "unsinkable."'
FROM 'THE DEATHLESS STORY OF THE *TITANIC*'
BY PHILIP GIBBS, 1912

On Tuesday 2 April 1912, the *Titanic* left Belfast to journey to Southampton from where she would begin her maiden voyage. Thousands gathered to wave goodbye to her.

The **Titanic** *at Southampton docks. The Captain and many of the crew were from Southampton.*

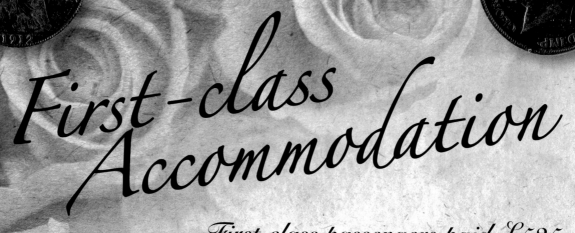

First-class Accommodation

First-class passengers paid £525 (£34,150 in today's money) for a ticket on the Titanic from Southampton to New York. If someone wanted one of the two staterooms, which included a 15m long private promenade deck, they cost £880 each.

As well as luxurious suites of up to five rooms, which included two bedrooms, two dressing rooms and a bathroom, there were also 350 cheaper standard first-class cabins with single beds.

A typical menu for first-class passengers.

One of the Titanic's first-class staterooms.

First-class passengers could make use of promenades on the 3 top decks, a swimming pool, gymnasium, Turkish and Electric baths, smoking rooms, a barbershop, library, racquet court and a Parisian-style restaurant.

The Titanic's Turkish baths.

Cafe Parisien was something new for ocean liners. It was designed to give diners the atmosphere of a Paris pavement cafe whilst, at the same time, large windows gave them a view of the sea as they dined.

In fine weather, Cafe Parisien's windows could be rolled down.

'But what a ship! ... Our rooms are furnished in the best of taste and most luxuriously and they are really rooms, not cabins.'

IDA R. STRAUS, FIRST-CLASS PASSENGER

First-class passengers enjoyed the best food, too. There were up to 11 courses at some meals and, on the evening of 14 April 1912, just hours before the ship's sinking, passengers enjoyed such delights as oysters, roast duckling, salmon, sirloin of beef, peaches in Chartreuse jelly, and vanilla and chocolate eclairs.

11

Second and Third-class Accommodation

There were 285 second-class passengers on board the Titanic: 157 men, 128 women and children. Cost of a ticket was £12.

WHITE STAR LINE.

R.M.S. "TITANIC."   APRIL 14, 1912.

THIRD CLASS.

BREAKFAST.
OATMEAL PORRIDGE & MILK
SMOKED HERRINGS, JACKET POTATOES
HAM & EGGS
FRESH BREAD & BUTTER
MARMALADE   SWEDISH BREAD
TEA   COFFEE

DINNER.
RICE SOUP
FRESH BREAD   CABIN BISCUITS
ROAST BEEF, BROWN GRAVY
SWEET CORN   BOILED POTATOES
PLUM PUDDING, SWEET SAUCE
FRUIT

TEA.
COLD MEAT
CHEESE   PICKLES
FRESH BREAD & BUTTER
STEWED FIGS & RICE
TEA

SUPPER.
GRUEL   CABIN BISCUITS   CHEESE
Any complaint respecting the Food supplied, want of attention or incivility, should be at once reported to the Purser or Chief Steward. For purposes of identification, each Steward wears a numbered badge on the arm.

A typical menu for third-class passengers. Food served in steerage was basic but nourishing.

Many third-class passengers (steerage) were emigrating to the United States from countries such as Ireland or Finland. In fact the passenger list for third-class listed 33 different nationalities. There were 712 people in third-class accommodation and a third-class ticket would have cost between £3 and £8. (In today's money £8 would be worth £536.)

Third-class passengers, Sarah Roth Witherson with Albert Iles; both survived the tragedy.

A second-class cabin.

It was said of the *Titanic* that the second-class accommodation was similar to first-class on other ships. Second-class cabins had two or four berths attached to the walls and were screened by curtains to give a little privacy. Sometimes the cabins would be booked by strangers who would share the cabin to bring down the cost of their tickets.

Cabins often held six bunks for family groups, or four bunks which could sometimes be slept in by four strangers all speaking different languages. Men were in the bow of the ship and women in the stern. The *Titanic*'s bunks were fitted with real mattresses plus blankets and pillows. Previously travellers in steerage would have slept on straw.

The third-class smoking room.

Bathing

There were only two bathtubs available for third-class passengers, one for the men and one for the women. This was not considered unreasonable as many people only bathed once a week and some thought that taking too many baths would give you lung disease.

Officers and Crew Members

Captain Edward J. Smith commanded the Titanic. He was 60 years old and had already commanded seventeen White Star Liners. Below Captain Smith in the chain of command were the Chief Officer, Henry Wilde and First Officer, William Murdoch. Second Officer Charles Lightoller had been shipwrecked before he joined the Titanic. On this occasion he was the highest-ranking officer to survive the sinking.

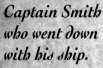

Captain Smith who went down with his ship.

The total number of crew members on board the *Titanic* when it sailed was 909. Sixty-six were employed on the decks as officers, storemasters and seamen. Nearly 500 were employed in the catering department as butchers, bakers, cooks, porters, pantrymen, storekeepers and restaurant staff. Other crew were instructors and attendants for the squash courts, gym and swimming baths, musicians and wireless operators.

The Titanic's gym.

Some of the officers who survived the Titanic's sinking.

There were 10 electricians and 25 engineers working on the *Titanic*. They were very well paid and it was their responsibility to make sure that the *Titanic*'s engines, generators and other machinery were in good working order.

Chief Officer Henry Wilde.

Men who worked in the *Titanic*'s six boiler rooms were known as the 'Black Gang'. Firemen shovelled coal into huge furnaces, which heated water in the boilers to produce steam. The speed of the ship then depended on the amount of steam that was allowed to enter the engines.

Setting Sail:
10 April 1912

By 8 am Captain Smith was on board ship making the final preparations for setting sail. Between that time and 12.15 pm when the Titanic was due to sail, boat trains brought the passengers to the dock where they were shown to their cabins by stewards. All third-class passengers were given medical checks before being allowed on board.

A family on board pose for a photograph.

WHITE STAR LINE

Soon after midday, when the Titanic cast off, she was escorted by tugs through Southampton Water. Then, when the *Titanic* passed by the liners *Olympic* and *New York* which were berthed nearby, the wash from the *Titanic*'s propellers led to the *New York* breaking free of her moorings and drifting out into the path of the *Titanic*. A collision was narrowly avoided but, to many, this incident seemed like another warning that all was not well with the ship.

A postcard of the RMS Titanic.

An artist's painting of the RMS Titanic on her maiden voyage.

Queenstown Southampton
Cherbourg
New York
Titanic

Map showing the Titanic's planned route to New York.

Lucky escapes

Some of the crew had gone ashore for the morning and were hurrying back before the ship sailed. Second-class passenger, Lawrence Beesley later wrote: 'Just before the last gangway was withdrawn, a knot of stokers ran along the quay...and made for the gangway. But a Petty Officer guarding the shore end of the gangway firmly refused to allow them on board.'

The First Few Days

Henry Wilde, Chief Officer of the *Titanic*.

The *Titanic's* maiden voyage took her first to Cherbourg, France, where 274 passengers joined the ship and 27 disembarked. From there she travelled to the port of Queenstown in Ireland (now called Cobh, close to Cork) where another 120 passengers joined the ship. Queenstown wasn't a big enough port for the *Titanic* to dock safely and so passengers and cargo were carried to the ship by tenders.

'I still don't like this ship... I have a queer feeling about it.'

CHIEF OFFICER HENRY WILDE WRITING TO HIS SISTER

At both ports, a number of mailbags were taken off the ship and others taken on. RMS *Titanic* stood for Royal Mail Steamer *Titanic* and the ship carried 3,423 mail sacks that contained more than 7 million items of mail.

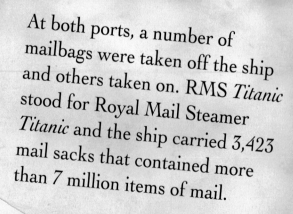

Lady Lucille Duff Gordon, one of the first-class passengers.

The *Titanic* left Queenstown at 1.30 pm on 11 April 1912 and set off on the Atlantic crossing to New York. There were 2,228 passengers and crew on board.

*The **Titanic**'s swimming pool.*

'I was up early before breakfast and met the professional racquet player in a half hour's warming up... (then) a swim in the six foot deep tank of saltwater heated to a refreshing temperature.'

COLONEL ARCHIBALD GRACIE, *TITANIC* SURVIVOR

The Rich and Famous

Many rich and famous people boarded the **Titanic** in Cherbourg.

Many rich Americans had booked to travel home on the Titanic. They had spent the winter in the south of France where the weather was warmer and by April it was time for them to return to the States. They mostly boarded the ship at Cherbourg accompanied by huge piles of luggage.

Mr Isidor Straus, the owner of Macy's, a large New York store, and his wife Ida, were on board along with Benjamin Guggenheim, a millionaire businessman; Mr George D Widener, son of a Philadelphia millionaire; and Mr. Washington Roebling, owner of a wire cable firm. Margaret 'Molly' Brown, a wealthy society lady from Denver, USA, would later be seen as a heroine for her efforts to help get people into the lifeboats when the ship was sinking, and for trying to pick up survivors.

The 'unsinkable' Molly Brown.

Among the English passengers were: Mr W. T. Stead, considered by many to be the greatest newspaperman of his age; Bruce Ismay, chairman of the White Star Line; and Thomas Andrews, the *Titanic*'s architect and managing director of Harland and Woolf.

Mr W.T. Stead had warned about liners being sent to sea short of lifeboats.

Titanic's millionaires *

Colonel J. J. Astor	£30,000,000
Mr B Guggenheim	£20,000,000
Mr I Straus	£10,000,000
Mr G Widener	£10,000,000
Mr W Roebling	£5,000,000

*in today's money these amounts would be 65 times as much.

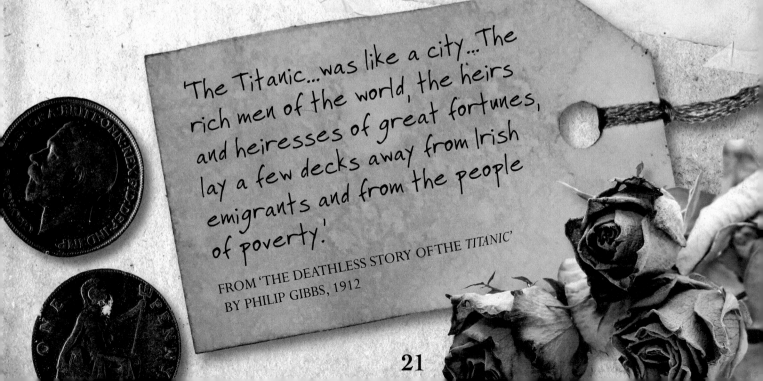

'The Titanic...was like a city...The rich men of the world, the heirs and heiresses of great fortunes, lay a few decks away from Irish emigrants and from the people of poverty.'

FROM 'THE DEATHLESS STORY OF THE *TITANIC*' BY PHILIP GIBBS, 1912

Icebergs Ahead

By 10 pm on 14 April 1912, many passengers on the Titanic were preparing to settle down for the night. Others were listening to the band or playing cards. The temperature outside was below freezing and warnings had been received indicating that there was ice close by.

One message, however, was not delivered to the officers on the ship's bridge. This warned of ice immediately in the path of the *Titanic*. Had this been received, then the *Titanic*'s speed would have been slowed.

Photograph of the iceberg that may have sunk the Titanic, taken April 15 1912.

The iceberg was estimated as being 55 to 60 feet above the water, which also meant that it would be 150 to 180 feet below the water. Spring is the worst time of year for icebergs in the Atlantic as they float south from the Arctic and into the paths of ocean liners. Icebergs are difficult to see at night if there is no moonlight and a calm sea means that waves cannot be heard splashing against them.

'Warning, iceberg right ahead.'

At 11.35 pm a warning was telephoned from watchers in the *Titanic's* crows nest saying that there was an iceberg head. First Officer Murdoch gave orders that the ship should turn to starboard and the engines go full speed astern and, although this prevented a head-on collision, the part of the iceberg that was hidden underwater caused severe damage to the ship's side when rivets gave way and the sea flooded in though gaps in the plates.

'It did not seem to me there was any great impact at all. It was as though we went over about a thousand marbles.'

MRS J STUART WHITE, FIRST-CLASS PASSENGER

The Wireless Room

Wireless equipment on the Titanic was both up to date and very powerful. It was operated by two radio officers, Jack Philips and his assistant, Harold Bride, who were under the command of Captain Smith, but employed by the Marconi Wireless Company.

Senior Marconi radio officer, Jack Philips.

'Just before midnight, Captain Smith came to the wireless room. Harold Bride recalled what he said: 'We've struck an iceberg,' he said, 'and I'm having an inspection made to tell what it's done to us. You'd better get ready to send out a call for assistance; but don't send it until I tell you.'

FROM 'THE DEATHLESS STORY OF THE *TITANIC*' BY PHILIP GIBBS, 1912

Harold Bride seated at the table in the wireless room.

Ten minutes later, Smith returned and ordered the signal to be sent. Philips tapped out the morse code for CQD - attention all stations - and then the *Titanic*'s radio call letters MGY. He also sent out a new distress call that had just come into use - SOS.

The signal was picked up by a number of ships that were all some distance from the *Titanic*, but then a message came in from the *Carpathia* to say that she was 58 miles away and heading towards the *Titanic*'s position as fast as she could, although it was estimated that it would take her four hours to get there.

No response

There was another ship, the *Californian*, closer to the *Titanic* but her wireless room had shut down for the night, so the distress calls were not received. Both Jack Philips and Harold Bride stayed in the wireless room sending out distress calls in the hope that they would be answered by ships that were nearer to the *Titanic*.

The wireless telegraph room.

Surely this Ship can't Sink?

Many passengers neither heard nor felt the collision with the iceberg and were woken only by noise in the corridors outside their rooms. Some passengers were woken by their stewards who encouraged them to get dressed and then go on deck.

**Mr Charles Lightoller,
Second Officer**

As they gathered on deck, everyone complained about the bitter cold and hoped they'd soon be back in their cabins. Second Officer Lightoller was off duty at the time and knew that his duty was to wait where he was until he was sent for. Fourth Officer Boxall eventually summoned him at 12.10 pm.

JACK PODESTA, A FIREMAN ON THE *TITANIC* WRITES IN HIS ACCOUNT OF THE DISASTER:

'Going back to our room, we began shaking one or two men up from their bunks. I said, "Come on Gus, get a lifebelt and go to your boat, she's sinking." He began laughing and simply lay back again, thinking it was a joke!'

The ship's architect, Thomas Andrews, who was onboard realised that there had been a major flaw in the design of the Titanic in that her watertight compartments were not high enough to prevent water flowing from one section to the next. He knew the ship was sinking; the only question was how long would it take to do so.

Damage caused by the collision affected five water-tight compartments.

As each compartment filled, the bow sank deeper, and water flowed over the top of the bulkheads. With five compartments flooded, the ship could not survive.

As more and more people began to crowd the decks, they were puzzled but not panicking. Officers ordered everyone to put on lifebelts. At that time distress rockets were being fired at five-minute intervals and at 12.25 am the order was given for women and children to be put into the lifeboats.

'We all walked up slowly with the lifebelts tied over our clothing, but even then we presumed that this was merely a wise precaution the captain was taking, and that we should return in a short time and go to bed.'

LAWRENCE BEESLEY, SECOND-CLASS PASSENGER

Women and Children first

At this point passengers began to realise how serious the situation was as they suddenly found out that husbands were to be separated from their wives.

Colonel J.J.Astor perished, but his wife was put on one of the lifeboats and survived.

The first boat lowered was only half full as officers believed that the boat might tip under the strain, but in the next hour and a half, 18 of the *Titanic*'s 20 lifeboats were successfully launched. Some of these were not fully loaded because of confusion as to who should go in the boats and the unwillingness of many wives to leave their husbands behind. Some were pushed or thrown into the boats while others clung onto the ship's railings.

Heartbreaking moments for families as the boats were filled.

The Goodwin family, third-class passengers, all of whom perished in the disaster.

'I heard Colonel Astor (an American millionaire) tell his wife that he would meet her in New York. They exchanged an affectionate farewell, but no more affectionate than that of a couple separating for a week instead of eternity.'

EDWARD WHEELTON, CHIEF STEWARD, QUOTED IN 'THE DEATHLESS STORY OF THE *TITANIC*' BY PHILIP GIBBS, 1912

Third-class passengers trying to find their way through to the upper decks, where the boats were being launched, were often held back by crew or found their way blocked by locked doors. By the time many of them made it through, most of the boats had been launched.

Death the Divider

Lost

Colonel J.J.Astor
Mr Penasco
Mr J.B.Thayer & Mr Thayer, Jr
Mr George Widener
Mr D. W. Marvin
Mr C.N. Hays
Mr Hart
Mr and Mrs Wick

Saved

Mrs Astor
Mrs Penasco
Mrs J.B.Thayer
Mrs G. Widener
Mrs D.W. Marvin
Mrs and Miss Hays
Mrs. Esther Hart and child
Miss Mary Wick

The Sinking Ship

The slant of the deck was getting steeper. Engineers were still frantically pumping out water to delay the ship from sinking, but at 1.20 am they were told to abandon their efforts and to try to save themselves.

Some of the lifeboats on board the Titanic.

At 1.45 am radio officer Jack Philips sent a final message to the *Carpathia* 'Come as quickly as possible, old man, engine room filling up to the boilers.' Shortly afterwards, Captain Smith told both Philips and Bride to abandon their posts, but both stayed on sending out messages until water started pouring through the door of the wireless room.

Many boats were launched
with empty places.

By 1.55 am only one boat
remained to be launched.
This was a collapsible
that the crew were having
difficulty with. It had 47
seats but there were still
over 1,600 people on board.

As the *Titanic* continued
to sink, passengers made
their way towards the
stern of the ship, which
was rising upwards out of
the water. Some passengers
had already started to jump
from the ship preferring to
take their chances in the sea.

*An artist's impression
of the sinking ship.*

Heroism

From the time that the first lifeboat was launched until ten minutes before the ship sank, the band members kept playing. Led by Mr Wallace Hartley they played selections from opera and some of the latest popular tunes, trying to keep people's spirits up. Their final piece of music was the hymn, 'Nearer My God to Thee'.

The brave members of the ship's band, none of whom survived.

'Many brave things were done that night but none more brave than by those few men playing minute after minute as the ship settled quietly lower and lower into the sea.'

LAWRENCE BEESLEY, *TITANIC SURVIVOR*

Heroic radio officers Philips and Bride were both picked from the water by the lifeboats. Bride survived but Philips died from hypothermia.

The Daily Graphic in its special *Titanic* memorial edition reported that Mr and Mrs Isidor Straus were drowned together. Mrs Straus had refused to leave her husband behind. 'We have lived together for many years. Where you go, I go.' Mrs Straus made sure that her maid, Miss Bird, was given a place in a boat and insisted on giving Miss Bird her shawl to help keep her warm.

Isidor Straus, owner of Macy's Store, New York

Mr Benjamin Guggenheim, millionaire and first-class passenger, went to his cabin when he knew the ship was sinking and changed into his finest clothes. Appearing back on deck with his manservant he was heard to say, 'We are dressed in our best and prepared to go down like gentlemen.'

Benjamin Guggenheim

Captain Smith... 'stood on the bridge and continued directing his men right up to the moment when the bridge on which he stood became level with the water. He then calmly climbed over the rail and dropped into the sea.'

LAWRENCE BEESLEY, *TITANIC* SURVIVOR

The Final Moments

Soon after 2 am the lights on the Titanic, which electricians had bravely struggled to keep working, flickered and then went out. Everything was now black.

Machinery, furniture and crockery could be heard crashing down through the ship as she slowly tilted on her end. Then came the noise of a huge explosion as the boilers burst and broke the ship in two.

Lady Duff Gordon who survived along with her husband.

'The stern rose 100 feet, almost perpendicularly, the boat standing up like an enormous black finger against the sky.'

LADY DUFF GORDON, *TITANIC* SURVIVOR. SURVIVORS REPORTED THAT THE SHIP STAYED IN THAT POSITION FOR SEVERAL MINUTES.

An artist's impression of the Titanic's final moments.

The front section of the ship sank almost immediately but the stern continued to rise and the forward funnel toppled over, crashing into the water and crushing swimmers under tons of steel.

'The oarsmen laid on their oars and all in the lifeboat were motionless as we watched her in absolute silence. Save some who would not look and buried their heads on each other's shoulders.'

LAWRENCE BEESLEY, TITANIC SURVIVOR

In a collapsible boat, J. Bruce Ismay, Director of the White Star Line Company, was one of those who couldn't bear to watch the ship disappear beneath the waves. As the stern sank, the Titanic seemed to pick up speed and at 2.20 am she vanished from sight.

Sketch by the 17-year-old John B. Thayer Jr, son of an American railroad businessman.

In the Lifeboats

Once the ship had gone down there were hundreds of people struggling in the icy water. The lifeboats had all rowed some distance away so that they wouldn't be sucked into the swell caused by the sinking ship and now there were voices calling through the night, begging the boats to return and pick them up.

A life jacket from the Titanic

'The sounds of people drowning are something that I cannot describe to you, and neither can anyone else. It's the most dreadful sound and there is a terrible silence that follows it.'

EVA HART, *TITANIC SURVIVOR*

Open to the elements, not all those in the lifeboats survived the freezing temperatures.

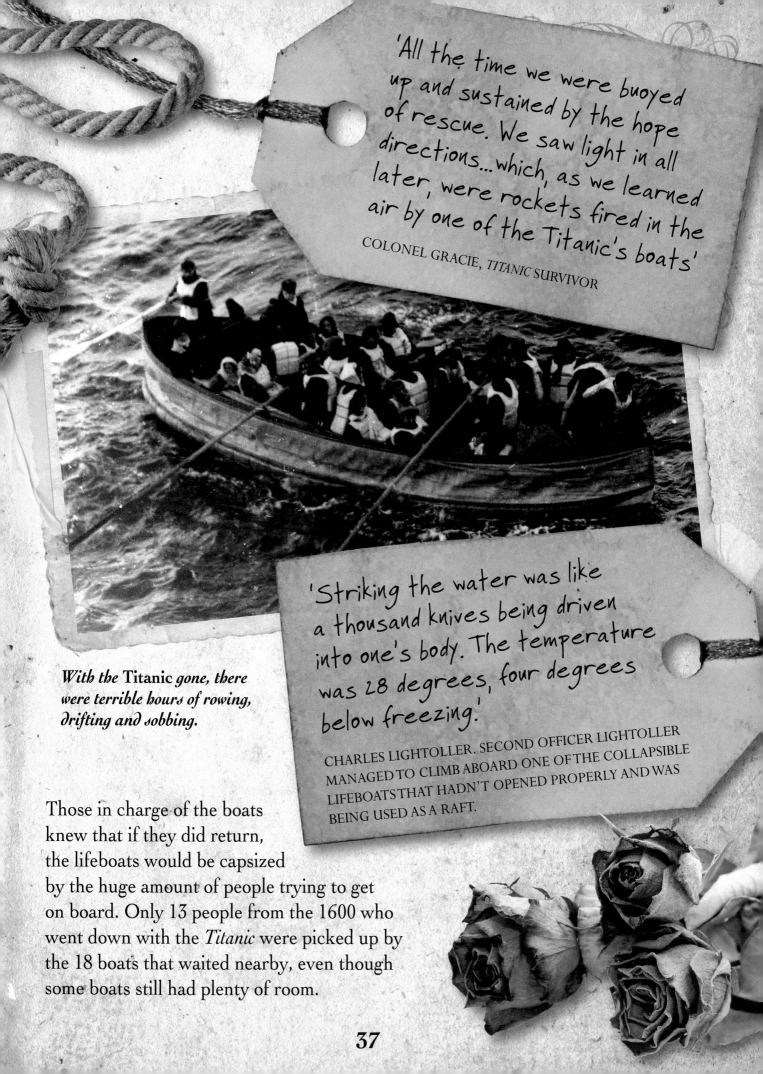

'All the time we were buoyed up and sustained by the hope of rescue. We saw light in all directions...which, as we learned later, were rockets fired in the air by one of the Titanic's boats'

COLONEL GRACIE, *TITANIC SURVIVOR*

'Striking the water was like a thousand knives being driven into one's body. The temperature was 28 degrees, four degrees below freezing.'

CHARLES LIGHTOLLER. SECOND OFFICER LIGHTOLLER MANAGED TO CLIMB ABOARD ONE OF THE COLLAPSIBLE LIFEBOATS THAT HADN'T OPENED PROPERLY AND WAS BEING USED AS A RAFT.

With the Titanic *gone, there were terrible hours of rowing, drifting and sobbing.*

Those in charge of the boats knew that if they did return, the lifeboats would be capsized by the huge amount of people trying to get on board. Only 13 people from the 1600 who went down with the *Titanic* were picked up by the 18 boats that waited nearby, even though some boats still had plenty of room.

Rescue

The commander of the Carpathia, Captain Rostron, had ordered full steam ahead from the moment he received the wireless report from the Titanic. However, he was travelling at night and through the same area of ice, and needed to alter course several times to avoid icebergs.

Titanic *survivors* alongside the rescue ship.

By 4 am the *Carpathia* had reached the *Titanic*'s last given position and soon after the first lifeboat was spotted. Dawn was breaking and very soon other boats could be seen.

'When day broke, I saw the ice I had steamed through during the night. I shuddered, and could only think that some other hand than mine was on that helm during the night.'

CAPTAIN ARTHUR H. ROSTRON, COMMANDER OF THE *CARPATHIA*

Captain Rostron, the Carpathia's commander.

Those survivors who had strength enough to climb rope ladders were taken aboard while others, exhausted, wet and chilled, had ropes tied round them to help hoist them up. Eva Hart, who was seven years old, tells how children were winched up in mail sacks, and that it was, 'terrifying, swinging about over the ocean.'

One man's feet had been crushed and frozen in the lifeboat.

Titanic *survivors on the deck of the* **Carpathia.**

'Deeply regret advise you TITANIC sank this morning after collision with iceberg, resulting in serious loss of life. Full particulars later.'

Telegram sent by J.Bruce Ismay, Director of the White Star Line

LAWRENCE BEESLEY TELLS OF HOW THE SURVIVORS IN HIS LIFEBOAT SAW A SINGLE LIGHT IN THE DARKNESS AND THEN A SECOND BELOW IT:

'It seemed almost too good to be true and I think everyone's eyes were filled with tears, men's as well as women's. All around us we heard shouts and cheers.'

Arrival in New York

Once all the survivors had been taken on board, Captain Rostron began searching the area for anyone else who might still have been alive. There were few traces of the ship - some floating chairs, cushions, rugs, lifeboats and just one body. By now other ships had reached the area and they began looking for bodies.

The New York Herald *reporting the tragedy.*

Once he was satisfied that no more could be done, Captain Rostron cancelled the *Carpathia*'s voyage to the Azores, turned the ship round and headed back to New York. There were 712 survivors on board.

'On arrival at New York everything possible was ready for our immediate assistance - clothing, money, medical aid and good accommodation, in fact, I think it would have been impossible for the people of America to have treated us better.

JOSEPH SCARROTT, *TITANIC* SURVIVOR

Hundreds of relatives and friends swarmed around the White Star offices in New York waiting for news, but very little came through from the *Carpathia*.

'To my poor fellow-sufferers: My heart overflows with grief for you all and is laden with sorrow that you are weighed down with this terrible burden that has been thrust upon us. May God be with us and comfort us all.'

ELEANOR SMITH, WIFE OF THE *TITANIC*'S CAPTAIN SMITH

Crowds waiting for news outside the White Star Line offices in London.

Lost and Saved

	First class Carried	Saved	Second class Carried	Saved	Third class Carried	Saved	Crew Carried	Saved
Men	173	58	160	13	454	55	875	189
Women	144	139	93	78	179	98	23	21
Children	5	5	24	24	76	23	-	-
Total	322	202	277	115	709	176	898	210

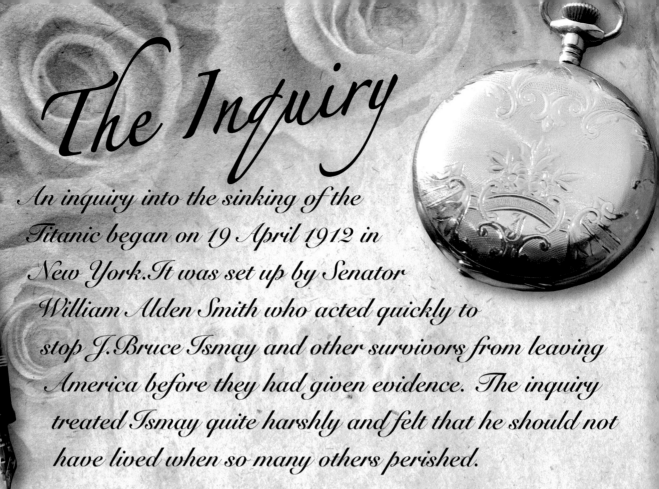

The Inquiry

An inquiry into the sinking of the Titanic began on 19 April 1912 in New York. It was set up by Senator William Alden Smith who acted quickly to stop J. Bruce Ismay and other survivors from leaving America before they had given evidence. The inquiry treated Ismay quite harshly and felt that he should not have lived when so many others perished.

A British inquiry was opened on 2 May and lasted till 3 July 1912. This also interviewed survivors along with shipbuilding and navigation experts. Both inquiries felt that there were many human errors - Captain Smith should not have allowed the ship to travel so fast where there was ice around, the ship's officers should not have allowed lifeboats to be launched half full.

J. Bruce Ismay being interviewed by the Senate inquiry in New York.

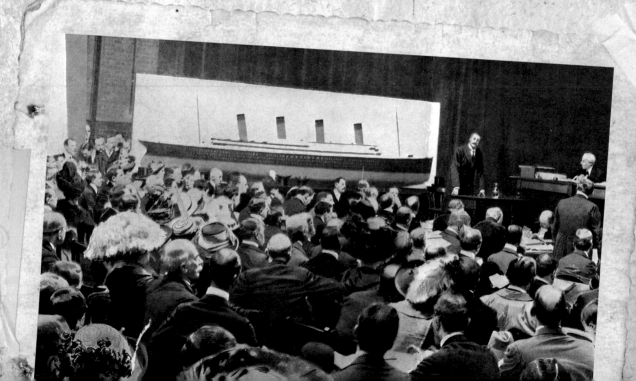

Sir Cosmo Duff Gordon being questioned about what happened in the lifeboats.

It was felt, however, that no one person was to blame for the tragedy. When Charles Lightoller was called to give evidence he claimed that everyone in charge behaved as they should have done. In his view the disaster was due to 'a combination of unlikely and unforeseeable circumstances.'

Captain Rostron being presented with an award, by Molly Brown, for his service in the rescue of the Titanic.

After the sinking of the *Titanic*, many more safety measures were put in place. Passenger ships were fitted with enough lifeboats to take everyone on board. Wireless rooms were to be manned at all times so distress calls would be picked up immediately. All ships carrying over 100 people were built with watertight inner hulls.

Discovering the Titanic

The Titanic sank in water that was over 2 miles deep and it wasn't until 1985 that a joint French and American expedition managed to locate her. This was led by Dr Robert Ballard and Jean-Louis Michel who found the ship 13 miles from her last recorded position.

The prow of the **Titanic**

They used sonar equipment to locate the vessel and then explored it with a video camera attached to a remote controlled vehicle. Ballard went back a year later and was able to reach the wreck himself in a submersible named 'Alvin'.

Pictures showed that the *Titanic* had indeed split in two. The bow section was found about 600 metres from the stern. He found that trailing rust covered much of the metal and that the wooden parts of the ship had been eaten away. Debris from the ship was scattered over a huge area.

An exhibit at the National Maritime Museum, Greenwich showing the submersible Nautile.

One of the survivors, Millvina Dean, who was only nine weeks old at the time, spoke out about disturbing anything, 'The ship is its own memorial. Leave it there.'

A submersible taking photographs of the wreck.

Over the years there have been various plans to try to raise the *Titanic* but it is now considered to be in far too poor a state for anything like that to be attempted. Ballard didn't disturb the wreck as he, too, thought it would be a kind of grave robbing, but since that time many objects have been recovered from the wreck including cutlery, plates, mugs, clothes found inside suitcases, shoes and even the ship's whistle.

45

Glossary

architect a designer of ships for the Royal Navy

astern towards the stern (rear)

boat trains trains that take passengers to ships

boilers huge tanks where water is heated to produce steam.

bow front end of a ship

bulkheads walls separating different compartments

chartreuse a green or yellow liqueur drink, made from herbs

collapsible something that can be folded up and stored flat

funnels hollow, cone-shaped metal tubes for the escape of smoke or steam.

furnaces very hot places where coal is heated

generators a machine for producing steam or electricity.

hull the main frame or body of a ship.

hypothermia very low body temperature

keel a structure running lengthways along the centre of the bottom of a ship

leviathan a monstrous beast, a sea monster

lough a loch (lake) in Ireland. (In this instance the Lagan is a sea lough, a narrow bay.)

naval gantry a framework in the form of a bridge, used to support a crane

petty officer a junior officer in the Navy

rivet bolt for fastening metal plates. Once put through a hole, the end is beaten flat.

stern rear end of a ship

starboard the right side of a ship when facing the bow (front)

stokers people employed to look after a furnace and keep it burning

tender a small boat that carries passengers and supplies to and from a bigger ship

the Ritz a luxurious London hotel

wireless another word for radio

On the trail of the Titanic

BELFAST, NORTHERN IRELAND - where the *Titanic* was built. It has a memorial that stands outside City Hall.

SOUTHAMPTON - where the *Titanic* began her maiden voyage. There is an exhibition about the ship and its passengers in the Maritime Museum. Also, around the city there are memorials to the *Titanic* postal workers, the *Titanic* musicians, the *Titanic* engineer officers and the *Titanic* crew (now in Holyrood Church). There is also a *Titanic* memorial just inside Dock Gate 4 (seek permission to visit from the security check point). Permission is also needed to visit the *Titanic*'s berth.

The Titanic memorial in Belfast.

QUEENSTOWN (now **COBH**) in Cork, Ireland. This was the *Titanic*'s last port of call before setting out across the Atlantic. The Queenstown Story, housed in Cobh Heritage Centre, tells about Irish emigration to America and includes a section on the *Titanic*.

MARYPORT, Cumbria. Here, visitors can follow the Ismay trail. Thomas Ismay, founder of the White Star Line, and his son J. Bruce Ismay, were born here. The Maritime Centre has photographs from Robert Ballard's expedition to locate the *Titanic*.

DALBEATTIE, SCOTLAND - has a memorial outside the Town Hall, to commemorate the heroism of First Officer William Murdoch who lost his life in the tragedy.

GREENWICH, LONDON - the National Maritime Museum has a permanent exhibition about the *Titanic*.

Index